MOTHERS OF
IRELAND

SOUTHERN MESSENGER POETS

Dave Smith, Series Editor

MOTHERS OF IRELAND

poems

JULIE KANE

LOUISIANA STATE UNIVERSITY PRESS

BATON ROUGE

Published by Louisiana State University Press
Copyright © 2020 by Julie Kane
All rights reserved
Manufactured in the United States of America
First printing

Designer: Barbara Neely Bourgoyne
Typeface: Adobe Garamond Pro
Printer and binder: LSI

Library of Congress Cataloging-in-Publication Data

Names: Kane, Julie, 1952– author.
Title: Mothers of Ireland : poems / Julie Kane.
Description: Baton Rouge : Louisiana State University Press, [2020] | Series:
    Southern messenger poets
Identifiers: LCCN 2019036529 (print) | LCCN 2019036530 (ebook) | ISBN
    978-0-8071-7075-5 (paperback ; alk. paper) | ISBN 978-0-8071-7314-5 (pdf) |
    ISBN 978-0-8071-7315-2 (epub)
Subjects: LCGFT: Poetry.
Classification: LCC PS3611.A544 M68 2020 (print) | LCC PS3611.A544 (ebook) |
    DDC 811/.6—dc23
LC record available at https://lccn.loc.gov/2019036529
LC ebook record available at https://lccn.loc.gov/2019036530

In memory of the strong women before me:

Hanora O'Connell McCarthy
Mary Hurley Lynch
Johanna Hennessey O'Brien
Mary Donovan Spillane
Mary Farty Carr
Julia Crowley Glynn
Isabella Manent Browne
Ellen Collins O'Kane

Mary "Minnie" McCarthy Lynch
Margaret O'Brien Spillane
Ellen Carr Glynn
Sarah Mary Browne O'Kane

Catherine Helen Lynch Spillane
Julia Agnes Glynn Kane

Nanette Spillane Kane

CONTENTS

ACKNOWLEDGMENTS

The author is grateful to the editors of the following publications in which these poems first appeared, sometimes in a slightly different form:

2 Bridges Review: "I Dreamed of Being Mothered by a Cat" and "Mornings, My Grandmother"; *Alabama Literary Review,* "The Scream"; *Atlanta Review:* "Whore"; *Birmingham Poetry Review:* "Arson in Knockmullane"; *Cherry Tree:* "As If," "At the Women's Clinic," "His Dream," "Tunnel of Light," and "You Were So Good"; *Dark Horse:* "To Tame a Feral Cat"; *Del Sol Review:* "Impatience Sonnet"; *Drunken Boat:* "Family Dramas"; *Gris-Gris:* "Burgers Fried in Salt"; *Hopkins Review:* "Petit Mal"; *Ithaca Lit:* "Giving Away the Liquor Bottles"; *Letters to the World: Poems from the Wom-Po Listserv:* "Aldie Street"; *Levure Littéraire:* "The Johns"; *Literary Matters:* "Second Time Around" and "That One Over"; *The Mackinac:* "Her Heart" and "Statue of Mary's Mother"; *The Maple Leaf Rag Anthology 5:* "Rotten Irish Teeth"; *Mezzo Cammin:* "Mother/Monarch"; *Peacock Journal:* "A Pair of Nylon Stockings"; *Poetry Net:* "My Great-Aunt Grace"; *Raintown Review:* "AA Story"; *Rainy Day:* "The Good Women"; *Rattle:* "Dullahan"; *Southern Quarterly:* "God Assembly Instructions" (as "Childhood's Space"); *Think Journal:* "Foxboro Sestina"; *Xavier Review:* "St. Joseph's #2, New Orleans."

"As If" was reprinted in *Best American Poetry 2016,* guest-edited by Edward Hirsch.

"The Good Women" was reprinted in Norton's *The Seagull Reader: Poems,* edited by Joseph Kelly.

"I Dreamed of Being Mothered by a Cat" was reprinted in *Love Affairs at the Villa Nelle,* edited by Marilyn L. Taylor and James P. Roberts.

MOTHERS OF IRELAND

THE GOOD WOMEN

Three out of four
are named Mary,
these good Irish women
who surface at wakes
like earthworms after rain.
Death makes them bake
turkeys, casseroles,
applesauce cakes.
They breathe the thick
incense of flowers
for strength, dispense
prayers like milk
from each massive breast.
Black becomes them.
Red-haired, broad-hipped
for easy babies,
I stand among them,
betrayer of my race:
I whose God bless you's
have no authority behind them
am awkward as the corpse
in this army of grace.

(1973)

I

IRELAND, MOTHER IRELAND

Oh, perfect loving mother,
Your exiled children all
Across the sund'ring seas to you
In fond devotion call.

—RAYMOND LOUGHBOROUGH AND
P. J. O'REILLY (1922)

INHERITANCE

They say that trauma's coded in the genes,
passed down to generations yet unborn
as thymine bases bond to adenines

and guanines throw a rope to cytosines
and brand-new double helixes are formed
with ancient trauma coded in the genes.

To watch one's children, with their mouths stained green
from eating grass till all the grass is shorn,
die one by one: do thymines, adenines

absorb the echoes of a parent's screams?
Too late, the boats of stony Indian corn.
Small wonder trauma's coded in the genes.

Like spools of film with horror movie scenes
in which our own progenitors performed,
those spiral loops of thymines, adenines

roll on inside us, soundless and unseen.
There's no escape, except not being born
from trauma not our own but in our genes:
The Hunger, coffin ships, 1916.

ARSON IN KNOCKMULLANE: 24 DEC. 1846

Patrick and Mary Horgan Lynch

Who'd burn a family's house down Christmas Eve,
the first year of the Famine? Men he knew,
who shoveled dirt beside him, men who heaved

great stones to lay the roadways, men aggrieved
he'd given up his land to join their crew—
the men who burned his house down Christmas Eve.

Because he had a roof of sod and sheaves
of straw while they lay down in ditch or pew,
they slunk up with a flaming torch, and heaved.

Six children slumbering. Their mother's sleeves
caught fire as she pulled out the youngest, two
weeks past his christening. That Christmas Eve,

the Inishannon jail was full of "thieves"
who'd stolen so they'd get a cell and soup.
The workhouse doors were bolted. How to heave

a baby in burned arms? Did they believe
in God and bless the dark that hid the view
of corpses in the road that Christmas Eve,
dead mouths stained green from eating grass and leaves?

THAT ONE OVER

Mary McCarthy Lynch (1867–1949)

She wore the china cabinet key around her neck
As if she couldn't trust even her longtime mate
To keep from making off with a gold-rimmed plate
To hock for whiskey money when he'd spent his check.
And what was inside the cabinet, to warrant theft?
China with chipped edges, "silver" that was silver plate,
A cut-crystal jam jar she grandly called a "vase,"
A statue of Mary that a Lourdes priest had blessed.
Everyone else in town thought her man hung the moon:
She wouldn't even call him by his Christian name.
"That one over," she'd say, pointing across the room.
She made him sleep on the porch when he'd had a few.
To be Irish then was to be awash in shame.
He hadn't deceived her yet, but you never knew.

SECOND TIME AROUND

Back when I used to smoke, I'd stub them out
in crystal ashtrays all around the house

that turned my stomach, emptied in the trash.
Times when I slipped the last one from the pack

too late at night to risk a run for more
at some gas station slash convenience store,

I'd comb through ashes for the longest butts
and light them up again without disgust.

Minnie McCarthy scandalized the town
of Knockmullane, Cork, turning Jack Lynch down.

Pretty girls wanted American fun,
not boredom in Ireland with a farmer's son!

He followed her over and found her on her knees
scrubbing Protestant toilets for a couple bucks a week

and proposed to her again with no resistance met.
He was the longest butt she was going to get.

HER HEART

Julia Margaret Lynch Curtin (1896–1939)

My grandmother's sister Julia was born with a flaw in her heart.

The doctor's words to her parents tore like a claw to the heart.

Head of her bed by a window, no winter thaw for the heart.

Never to wed because childbirth would be the last straw for her heart.

Rumors her father punched at least one suitor's jaw for her heart.

But a redheaded traveling salesman would not withdraw from her heart.

Swearing his love was chaste and he'd keep hands off for her heart.

Swearing on Mary and Jesus with one freckled paw on his heart.

How could her bantamweight father not go soft in the heart?

Beautiful bride: such a chorus of ooh's and ah's from all hearts.

When her belly poked out it proved there is no law to the heart.

Julia's motherless boys would grow up raw in the heart.

THE JOHNS

Julia Agnes Glynn Kane (1890–1970)

It's true that my Grandma Agnes named three children John.

Living children, not dead: all bearing the name of John.

You might assume she was crazy about her husband, John.

But the truth is, following childbirth, she truly hated John.

Torn and bleeding, worn out, she'd put the blame on John.

When the nurse came around with the form, there'd be no sign of John.

Agnes would hiss at the nurse, "Oh, Christ! Just put down *John*."

Once she got home with the child, she'd grow attached to "John."

Then she'd begin to call him some name other than John.

But it caused some mix-ups at school that they were all named John.

And the draft board wasn't amused that they were all named John.

My Uncle Jim was the only son who was not named John.

He was named for Agnes's father, who was a James, not John.

James Glynn died on a mental ward surrounded by John Does.

Jim Kane was always a good boy, unlike the three bad Johns.

ST. JOSEPH'S #2, NEW ORLEANS

Gregory Browne (d. 6 Sep. 1878) and Kate Manning Browne (d. 5 Sep. 1878)

Dealers are trilling their lookout alarms
As I enter the city of the dead:
Row after row of gleaming marble tombs
In the middle of a bad neighborhood.

I am looking for Kate and Gregory Browne
Who died a day apart of yellow fever
Vomiting blood as black as coffee grounds
On Bourbon Street in the French Quarter.

Gregory was thirty, Kate twenty-five.
They would have been married two years at Christmas.
No record if they left behind a child,
My flesh-and-blood raised by charity sisters.

What drew them to this fever-ridden port,
Far away from any relative,
Doubly displaced from Galway and the North?
I had the excuse of marrying a native.

Foolish of me to think I'll find their names
Among grand temples to the Creole French.
Immigrant victims were dumped in mass graves,
Covered with lime in shallow dirt trenches.

Better get out of here before I'm robbed
Or find my Prius with the windshield smashed:
Not even rented space in oven-vaults
For poor Irish victims of Yellow Jack.

A pity no one searched their rented room,
Found an address, let distant family know.
All those years believing I was far from home,
So close to my great-grand-uncle's bones.

MY DOUBLE COUSIN ANNA

Anna Maria Hurley O'Mahony (1881–1972)

My double cousin Anna O'Mahony was a spy for her country.
She was Anna Hurley then, nearly forty, but not yet a bride for her country.

She would scout the British troops getting on and off trains at the Bandon
    depot.
Her farmhouse in Laragh stashed ammo and dispatches inside for her country.

One time she got raided and stuffed two IRA men under her dying father's bed.
"My father is dying in there: I pray you search quietly," she not-quite-lied for
    her country.

Anna's father Daniel, a Land League man, had named her "Anna" for Charles
    Parnell's sister.
Anna Parnell, unlike her brother, never compromised for her country.

Anna Hurley's brother was a captain in the Third West Cork Brigade.
Shot in the back by Black and Tans, Frank Hurley died for his country.

Was it Anna who planted the plain iron cross by the Bandon River footbridge?
Silent reminder of a good man crucified for his country.

John O'Mahony went on hunger strike in London's Wormwood Scrubs Prison.
A big man, starved for sixteen days, he managed to survive for his country.

After the war was over, her father and brother dead, Anna married O'Mahony.
He was her link to the time she'd been most alive for her country.

To think she was still alive, past ninety, when I backpacked through Ireland
    at twenty,
Believing that no one over thirty knew a thing about the fight for a country.

FAMILY DRAMAS

Act One: The Glynn-Kanes

Whatever time the "boys" got home for dinner,
Dinner would be ready, because something gray
Was always bobbing in a long slow simmer

On the gas stove next to the electric wringer
My aunt had won (for once) on opening day
Of the A&P that sold the meat for dinner,

Boiled past telling: Was it beef, or liver?
Now and then some washed-up horse or grey-
Hound won against long odds, and then the simmer

Of her long slow anger wouldn't breach the inner
Surface of the cookpot of her rage,
Though she'd slam down plates as she dished out dinner,

Grandma eating in her room, having lingered
Decades in her "sickbed" since her husband went away
And her heart boiled over from its long slow simmer.

Most nights they'd slink home losers or sinners:
Steak knives and teeth tearing into that gray
Sodden substance being served up for dinner,
Words trying edges on what had long simmered.

Act Two: The Lynch-Spillanes

Mary on the wall in my grandmother's room
With a holy palm frond stuck behind the frame
Looked like a hussy with an ostrich plume

In her hat, by the dresser with My Sin perfume
And a silver-backed brush; but the walls were quite plain
Across the hallway in my grandfather's room,

And even a child could safely assume
That the bedrooms and silences meant that some shame
Still lurked like a hussy in an ostrich plume.

Grandma made Mary Jane cocktails: one teaspoon
Of cherry juice making the ginger ale stain,
While Grandpa just yelled at us: "Go to your room,"

When we stepped in his garden or banged out of tune
On his precious piano. "Our room" was the same
That my mother had slept in—its Mary, too, plumed.

Past forty, I learned what they took to their tombs:
Once, sent home from school with stomach pains,
My mother found them in the living room,
Her mother and the priest, like a bride and groom.

Act Three: The Spillane-Kanes

We three little girls would be sent outside
(She liked to call the street a "cul-de-sac")
Whenever the two of them had to fight,

Although we were in our rooms the night
She shattered glass after glass after glass
On the bricks around the fireside—

Clutching our teddy bears, terrified—
And even then, their words were held back.
Whenever the two of them had to fight,

We'd take our bikes for a good long ride
Or play with our trolls or Mouse the cat,
And it could get dark and cold outside.

We, too, had truths we had to hide:
The times he begged for a loan of cash
From our china pigs (we knew they'd fight

If we told), the times she cried and cried,
And dinner was milk and Sugar Smacks.
Although we were always sent outside,
Their words still burned like dead stars' light.

Act Four: The Cavan-Tyrones

I read that play in high school. Mrs. T.
Took morphine, but I knew the family well:
The language of their fights like poetry,

The silences like wind through stunted trees,
The drunken charmers and the ne'er-do-wells
Who couldn't charm the bitter Mrs. T.

The backdrop of a gray Atlantic sea,
As cold in August as a heart withheld,
Its rhythms those of Irish poetry—

O'Neill's own family drama spoke to me,
"The ponies" running like a carousel
Whose painted glitter holds out mystery

But finish line becomes infinity,
How habits shape of lives a villanelle,
The repetitions turned to poetry.

I pray to the quatrain to set me free;
We Irish know that language is a spell.
I read that play in high school, Mrs. T.
My fate without the grace of poetry.

STATUE OF MARY'S MOTHER

There is no God, and Mary is his mother.
—attributed to George Santayana

She does not take communion on the rare occasions when she finds herself at Mass for a Catholic wedding or funeral, yet she has four images of Mary in her bedroom—five, if you count the lumpy baby Mary being held by her mother, Saint Anne. That little china statue belonged to her grandmother—not the pretty, flirty Gram who was the president of her local altar society, but the other one, with stringy gray hair and nicotine-stained fingers, who lay in bed shrieking curses at the assholes on Boston talk radio. That grandmother, who lost her mother to cancer as a girl, wanted to be a nightclub singer, until she got knocked up in her teens and had to get married. She left the Church when an Irish housemaid aunt with a nest egg died and willed it all to Catholic charities. But she didn't get rid of the religious statue: she just rolled it up in a soft towel and stashed it in a bureau drawer. Mary is always a baby when portrayed with her mother, because she was three years old when handed over to the temple priests. Did Saint Anne feel sad? Or merely smug at having done her duty? Her likeness stares straight ahead, the gaze unreadable. One hand cups the baby's bottom, and the other points to heaven.

II

A MOTHER'S LOVE'S
A BLESSING

A mother's love's a blessing
No matter where you roam
Keep her while she's living
You'll miss her when she's gone

—THOMAS PETER KEENAN (1866–1927)

ALDIE STREET

She still has nightmares of that third-story window
Through which her mother leans to hang the laundry
With brown wooden clothespins on a pulley-fed line
Between two tenement apartments in Boston.
One minute she's screaming in her mother's lap,
And the next, she's plummeting down to the sidewalk.

Her bean-thin father comes striding up the sidewalk
And her black-haired mother spies him from the window.
Reaching for a bottle of cologne, her mother slaps
Two drops behind her ears, abandons the wet laundry,
And thinks about going to a jazz club in Boston.
They can get there and back on the green subway line.

But what about the child? They have to realign
Their priorities. The Italian widow across the walk
Might sit with the infant for one night in Boston.
They look out the window to see her lighted window,
Her clothesline of cone-bra and housedress laundry
Against which a Charles River breeze begins to slap.

Later, the baby wakes with the croup. Her mother slaps
Her on the back, but she can't breathe, so her father makes a beeline
For the tub, runs the hot water, and dangles her like laundry
Over the steaming cauldron. *Put me down, let me walk,*
The baby's thinking. Through the fogged-up bathroom window,
Snow falls on the Popsicle laundry of Boston.

The dead do not always stay buried in Boston.
One weekday, hanging laundry, the child's mother slaps
Her own mouth to see a ghost appearing out the window—
Her father-in-law. She had fallen for the line
That the old man was dead, but there he was on the sidewalk,
Dying of prostate cancer, a stick hung with laundry,

Coming to see his grandchild, swaddled in laundry,
Before being buried in the stony ground of Boston,
A latter-day wise man at the end of his walk.
"You lied to me," the child's mother cries as she slaps
Her drunk husband that night, who can't walk a straight line,
Though he claims he "worked late" as she paced by the window.

Airing her dirty laundry, her mother says, "I slapped
You so hard, once, in Boston, my hand left a line;
How I longed, as I walked you, to hurl you out that window."

MOTHER/MONARCH

Nanette Spillane Kane (1926–1995)

You with your brown pantsuits and flat shoes, so sensible;
Who would have guessed you'd come back as a butterfly?
But something in your house was always burnt orange:
A sofa, the basement walls, one zigzag in the collage
Of genuine South American butterfly wings
Whose artist must have been a heartless little shit.

None of your second-graders would dare say "shit"
In your classrooms—not if they were the least bit sensible.
But even the worst boys got a kick out of seeing wings
Emerge from jade-earring cocoons of monarch butterflies
Gathered each fall along roadside ditches collaged
With leaves colored red, yellow, brown, and orange.

My favorite high school minidress was striped black and orange.
I thought I looked "groovy," but I must have looked like shit.
I believed that a high hemline or low décolletage
Could save me from your fate of being drab and sensible.
The year I turned sixteen, I hatched into a butterfly.
In the back seats of Beetles, boyfriends pinned my new wings.

Between your force and my face, only a guardian angel's wings,
When rage at my rebelliousness made you see orange.
Your pretty young Irish mother had been a flirt, a social butterfly;
The grumpy old man she married, a bit of a shit.
You sided with him in the war of beauty versus the sensible.
Those were your mother's silks and powders, glued in your collage.

We propped it on the nursing home windowsill, that collage,
During the last weeks of your dying, when black and orange wings
Kept crashing into my windshield. I'd tell myself to be sensible;

Then I'd walk out into a parking lot and see a flash of orange
Lying in the gravel, bird-pecked, decaying like shit.
Soon your soul would fly out of your mouth, an Egyptian butterfly.

The winter after you died, twenty million monarch butterflies
Perished in a freak Mexican snowfall, their corpses collaged
On tree trunks in volcanic mountains, their beauty turned to shit.
How many canvases would you have papered with those wings?
Were you striking my face from beyond, by killing all that orange?
I write it down as if language could make it sensible.

A PAIR OF NYLON STOCKINGS

> But she went on feeling the soft, sheeny luxurious things—
> with both hands now, holding them up to see them glisten,
> and to feel them glide serpent-like through her fingers.
> —Kate Chopin, "A Pair of Silk Stockings"

My mother washed her stockings all at once.
The bathroom was a cave on nights they hung

Stalactite-like and dripping. I had one
Lone pair and prayed to God they wouldn't run

(Long hours of babysitting neighbor brats
My way of earning the replacement cash).

The only stocking color I could buy
To not be outcast from my junior high

Was "Cinnamon." My red-brown legs would clash
Bizarrely with the rest of my pale flesh,

But all we teenage girls had legs that matched
And we conformists were relieved at that.

That whiff of acetone when someone dabbed
Clear polish on a run to stop its tracks,

Right in the middle of algebra class:
The odor filled our lungs like mustard gas.

My mother saw conspiracies. She swore
That stockings never ran before the war,

When nylon went to making parachutes.
"Those chemists *made* them run, to rake in loot,"

She'd hiss. But she had more than she could wear,
Still in their packaging, to my one pair.

Those times I'd buy a brand unknown to me,
Only to find they only reached mid-knee;

Those black mascara tears I used to cry—
These days, even a death can leave eyes dry.

I washed my stockings in the bathroom sink
Before I went to bed at night, and cringed

On mornings they were damp against my skin.
Imagine buying stockings on a whim!

I could afford to now, but I don't care,
Teaching in sandals with my veined legs bare.

ROTTEN IRISH TEETH

1

DON'T FEED ME CANDY!
(Signs pinned to our coats by Mom.)
Name tags, she told us.

2

Wore my retainer
to school, as if I could get
an "A" in braces.

3

Dad was on TV.
They capped his top teeth, bright white.
Bottom row, yellow.

4

All Mom's top teeth pulled.
Her shame at the container
on the toilet lid.

5

Don't marry Irish,
she warned us Irish daughters.
And check out his teeth.

I DREAMED OF BEING MOTHERED BY A CAT

I dreamed of being mothered by a cat,
Sunk in her plush as in a featherbed.
I'd never known a happiness like that.

My human mother's claws would not retract.
Even her language could unzipper red.
I dreamed of being mothered by a cat

Who'd give her life to save me from attack.
I sensed that fierceness in her as I fed.
I'd never known a happiness like that.

If there were siblings, I ignored that fact.
I had her to myself (or I forget)
The whole time I was mothered by a cat.

One dream can strike you like a thunderclap.
That mother cat, more goddess than a pet.
I'd never known a happiness like that.

The world was pure sensation, not abstract:
Some realm between the living and the dead.
I dreamed of being mothered by a cat
And something healed inside me after that.

FOXBORO SESTINA

My mother just wanted to get out of Foxboro
Where it was embarrassing to be Irish Catholic.
The priest kept his golf clubs in her parents' shed,
A blanket excuse to drop in for a drink.
Everyone knew everyone else's secrets
In that town of ten thousand with its central green.

Mayflower descendants once grazed sheep on that green
Smack in the middle of downtown Foxboro
And it was a very badly kept secret
They'd burned down the first church built by Catholics
(So rinky-dink, its Crucifixion was only a painting).
Firemen just let it burn, as if it were some backyard shed.

Fires could have been quenched with the tears my mother shed.
Once, sent home from grade school with her stomach green,
She found her pretty young Irish mother drunk
In the lap of the duffer priest of Foxboro.
Seven years old, she began to hate being Catholic,
Though she kept what she saw that afternoon a secret.

How often she wished she could keep it a secret
That her Granny kept chickens in a coop behind the shed!
Protestants bought their chickens already plucked, unlike Catholics.
These days, it is cool to raise chickens and eat green,
But it was not cool when my mother lived in Foxboro.
She prayed they'd all drown in the trough where they drank.

My mother's Uncle Tim was the town's official drunk.
The brains of the family, Tim was rumored to have secretly
Taken the dental boards for his brother, in practice in Foxboro.
But once Tim started drinking, all inhibitions were shed.
He would serenade her friends from his spot on the town green:
Sad songs like "Kathleen Mavourneen," so embarrassingly Irish Catholic.

My mother escaped the town (though she raised us vaguely Catholic)
By marrying a dashing Irishman a bit too fond of drink.
For her 50th high school reunion, she returned to stand on its green,
Surprising us all with sentiment she'd managed to keep secret.
Did she sense the encroaching cancer, that looming watershed?
That last year, she drank from a mug that said "Foxboro."

IN THE END

Always so quick to strike with words or hand,
you were a different person in the end:
as if you had become a dying friend,
as if a general gave up his command.
And when you passed into that borderland
where your own house seemed strange as something dreamt,
the cancer ravaging your brain cells then,
you told my dad that I would understand.
Bad memories can't be erased, they say,
but can be written over. If that's true,
I'll concentrate on my last sight of you,
your parched lips forming the initial "J"
as I leaned down above your hospice bed
accepting your surrender, nearly dead.

BURGERS FRIED IN SALT

Once upon a time there was a wicked Queen who fried hamburger patties in salt: a giant patty for the King; a medium patty for herself; and three eeny-weeny patties for the three princesses. The burgers came out of the pan as black and as hard as lava rocks, because the salt leached all of the juices out of the meat. One day after the Queen had died of meanness, the oldest princess, to whom she had been the meanest, decided to fry a burger in nothing but its own juices. It was delicious! She didn't know that the middle princess, who had run away from home as soon as she was able, had been frying her burgers in big fat gobs of butter for years. But the youngest princess, who had squeezed a few dribs and drabs of love out of the Queen by being cute as a chipmunk when she was little, kept on frying her burgers in salt. That one gave birth to a daughter, loved even before she was born, who refused to eat any meat at all, saying that her dreams were haunted by milk cows bellowing for their stolen veal calves, and by slaughterhouse cattle bellowing for their long-lost mothers.

III

THE CRUEL MOTHER

She said, "Dear children, can you tell,"
Fal the dal the di do,
"Where shall I go? To heav'n or hell?"
Down by the green wood side.

—TRADITIONAL MURDER BALLAD

WHORE

What kind of mother calls her daughter "whore"
when she finds out her daughter's fiancé
is moving in a couple months before

the wedding? Small-town priggish to her core,
smug priest who slams shut the confessional grate:
that kind of mother calls her daughter "whore."

Yet, when that husband battered down a door,
came crashing through a bookshelf barricade,
the daughter phoned her mother just before,

instead of the police, or friends. What for?
The mother snapped, "Oh, don't exaggerate."
The phone line crackled with the unsaid "whore."

The daughter crumbled after the divorce.
She slept around as if each drunken lay
could blot out all the ugliness before:

so many men that she could not keep score.
They cradled her, if only till they came.
Once you have heard your mother call you "whore,"
you might as well be, if you weren't before.

YOU WERE SO GOOD

You were so good, you didn't make me sick
That first trimester that I carried you.
Not knowing there were two of us to feed,
I fed my change into the snack machine
Late afternoons at work, a change of habit.
Nights, TV couples joked about dead rabbits.

You were so good, you even let me bleed
That first trimester that I carried you.
The low-dose estrogen had made me spot
All month, so when I finally went off
And kept on spotting, never really flowing,
That's how I went so long without knowing.

You were so good, you must have been a girl
That one trimester that I carried you:
Trusting innately if you made no fuss,
Just kept your head down and were *good* enough,
I wouldn't let them cut you out like cancer.
I didn't ask your sex. I knew the answer.

HUNDRED-DOLLAR BILL

So crisp, it looked like he had ironed it,
That hundred-dollar bill he handed me.
So green, it looked like it was counterfeit,

Or manufactured for Monopoly.
So cool, as if he'd done it in the past,
The banknote ironed like his Izod tee.

It cost two hundred, so he gave me half.
His hand was massive as a catcher's mitt:
Pink on one side and on the other, black.

I kept the bill I should have given back.

AT THE WOMEN'S CLINIC

They had us all breathe into paper bags
So that we wouldn't hyperventilate.
Like ponies with our snouts in feeding sacks,
We kept our heads down. During the day's wait,
They made us list our reasons to keep it.
A married woman with four children cried.
Doubting if any of the staff would read it,
I wrote, "To understand justice denied."
At last, my heels were planted in stirrups,
The speculum inserted, my cervix numbed.
But something was wrong. The doctor's terseness:
"Looks like you're farther along by a month.
Get up, get dressed." New plans would be arranged.
Twelve weeks along and the fathers had changed.

PETIT MAL

"We could get married," I said, but I made him sick:
Not anything anyone else would notice,
Just a spell of petit mal that lasted seconds
But left him temporarily at a loss for words.

Not anything anyone else would notice,
But triggered more frequently at times of stress.
When he dumped me, it left me at a loss for words.
My life then was one big ball of chaos:

My workplace mired in scandal, my ex triggering stress
Late nights when he battered his weight against the door.
My life then was one big ball of chaos,
But a good man had loved me for almost three months.

I slept at his place to escape the assaults on my door.
Breakfast was home-baked bread with apple butter.
A good man, he loved me for almost three months.
When his bathroom was a darkroom, I had to hold my pee.

Coffee in bed, and bread with apple butter.
I was so happy with him, I knew it couldn't last.
He wore old-lady underpants and sat on the john to pee.
His pickup truck was orange, his sneakers full of kittens.

I was so happy with him, I knew it couldn't last.
It had been over since March when I had to tell him,
Sobbing in the cab of his burnt-orange truck,
That I was three months pregnant and he was the father.

It had been over since March when I had to tell him
(Triggering a petit mal seizure that lasted seconds)
That I was three months pregnant and he was the father.
"We could get married," I said, but I made him sick.

HIS DREAM

The night before, he dreamed about a mouse
Clinging to a vacuum cleaner wand.
Its paws were braced on the rim of the hose.
It held its own in that tornado wind.
He told it to me in his pickup truck.
Once heard, a dream like that becomes your own.
He was driving me to the women's clinic,
Shaken up by the past night's omen.
There was one moment, in that pre-dawn ride,
Trying not to think of the struggling mouse,
I might have been able to change his mind.
But always, in nightmares, no sound comes out
And the next thing I knew, the pickup swerved.
A careful driver, he had jumped a curb.

COUPLED

We were no longer a couple, but we were a sort of family.
We spent the following Thanksgiving together.

Potluck in a bar on stilts above a Galveston beach.
Just for that long weekend, we were living together.

And once, in the early nineties, when he passed through New Orleans,
We met in PJ's Coffee, hugged, clinging together.

If the universe does branch off each time a decision is made,
There are planets on which we need no forgiving together.

Julie, he said, *I just assumed there'd be other children.*
Bound by a red silk thread to be parents of nothing forever.

TUNNEL OF LIGHT

Those who return report that, at the end
Of the tunnel of light, there's a receiving line
Made up of dead loved ones: relatives, not friends,
Blocking the gate to whatever lies behind.
It could be from a lack of oxygen,
A shared illusion as the brain cells die,
But it will still feel like it's genuine,
No matter if it's real or one last lie.
My mother waits there in her spider web:
No way around except by going through.
My little lost infant waits in her crib.
I don't fear dying, but I fear those two.
O holy mother, help us to forgive
Those who killed us and those who let us live.

IV

THE PARTING GLASS

And all I've done for want of wit
To memory now I can't recall
So fill to me the parting glass
Good night and joy be with you all

—TRADITIONAL FOLK SONG

MORNINGS, MY GRANDMOTHER

Catherine Helen Lynch Spillane (1901–1963)

Mornings, my grandmother lingered in bed,
Reading her missal with mother-of-pearl
Covers. On visits, I'd fling my leg

Up over the blankets. Jesus bled
On a medical cross with bandages curled
Inside. My grandmother lingered in bed.

Pictures of Mary hung overhead.
Back of each frame, a palm unfurled
From past Palm Sundays. I'd fling one leg

Up over the side as my grandmother read.
A chestnut tree was buzzing with squirrels
Through lace curtains. She lingered in bed.

I am no girl, and my grandmother's dead,
Waiting in light at the edge of the world.
Hungover mornings, I've flung my legs

Up over men's shoulders, thought in dread
Of the previous nights when the rooms whirled,
Wished I believed what my grandmother read
Sweet holy mornings she lingered in bed.

DULLAHAN (BLACKOUTS)

With pity for all living things
Being chased by a ghoul on a horse
With its head tucked under its arm
Consider the plight of the rider

Consigned to blank nights on a horse
Or behind the wheel of an automobile
Consider the plight of the rider
Cruising the potholed streets of your city

Headless inside her automobile
Sheer muscle memory steering her home
Cruising the potholed streets of your city
Dullahan, headless Irish fairy

Drone-like, mindless, riding home
You may have sensed her, late one night
Dullahan, headless Irish fairy
Caught up in repetition

You may have sensed her, many nights
With your shamed red face in your hands
Caught up in repetition
With pity for all living things

GOD ASSEMBLY INSTRUCTIONS

Once you were happy gluing Popsicle sticks,
Folding toilet-tissue roses for a Mother's Day corsage

You must try to get back to that space in your childhood
Where your mind put no limits on creation

You need not be talented at building things
You must patch it together as best you can

From those moments of grace you're unable to explain
By a spin of the wheel in a board game

When you pray, you will breathe life into it
You may pray to the earth-made moon, if you wish

Pray to anything except your own name

TO TAME A FERAL CAT

I'll tell you how to tame a feral cat.
(Before I learned, I scared away a few.)
You're going to have to be the first to act:
A feral cat will never come to you.
A can of tuna fish is best, though not
A steady diet of it, as it's rich.
You'll have to hide so you will not be caught
Or it will figure that the meal's a trick.
Once it gets used to eating without fear,
Step out and let it see you: it will run.
The sixth or seventh time that you appear,
The cat will let you stay until it's done.
Now's when you have to start to baby-talk,
Though it will startle when it hears your voice;
But pretty soon the noise won't run it off.
Say anything at all. It's not your choice
Of wording, but the tones the cat will hear.
Try stepping closer with an outstretched palm.
Before too long, the cat will let you near,
Still crooning to it in a sort-of-psalm.
Once it accepts your nearness as a fact,
Reach out and touch its fur. Electric shock
Would not so startle it, and this bold act
Is very likely to set back the clock.
Don't be discouraged when the cat withdraws.
Prepare to wait: the cat will come around.
All of a sudden, when you speak and pause,
The cat will answer with a plaintive sound,
Again, again—you'll know it isn't chance
But give-and-take you both can understand.
The cat will move its body in a dance
And arch its back to meet your human hand.

So when they told me, in my drinking days,
I had to find a god or I would die,
I hid my doubts and took a leap of faith.
I knew one certain thing: that it and I
Were different species. With the age of signs,
Of symbol-language spelled in flames or doves
Long over, any first move would be mine;
And the response, if any, would be Love's.

GIVING AWAY THE LIQUOR BOTTLES

Home from college one Christmas, I packed
My dolls away in cardboard boxes,
Shutting their eyelids and smoothing their skirts
For the long sleep through time

Under the eaves of my parents' house.
How easily attachments go!
A moth flies out of the corpse's mouth.
In the end, we are dolls ourselves.

It was the same with my wedding dress
The day I gave it to Goodwill.
Do pharaohs wake in their tombs to find
Their jewels mean nothing to them?

Each step prepares us for the next.
Each loss prepares us for the last.
The hardest dolls to lose were glass,
That carton of outworn friends.

AA STORY

Across a hundred rooms with kiddie chairs,
Throughout a hundred mumbled AA prayers,
I wondered if your hugs were chaste as theirs.
Or tighter, closer?

You told your story once: old wealth, Tulane,
Those clubby breakfasts at the Pontchartrain,
Then begging on the beach for pocket change
In Pensacola.

Some nights we wound up partners, playing cards
In coffee shops we hung out in like bars.
You never knew if diamonds outranked hearts
Or hearts beat diamonds.

And once, because my car was in the shop,
You said you'd pick me up and drop me off.
You leaned so close to me, your breath felt hot
On my bare shoulder.

Who would have guessed we two would fall in love,
Or last until Katrina screwed it up?
Eleven years, three parents gone to dust,
And us still sober.

And now the time apart begins again,
Like film run backward, or a repetend
From fixed poetic form, and in our end
Is our beginning.

IMPATIENCE SONNET

Hanging on crutches at my screened back door,
I spot my paper lying in the grass
And hope my balance isn't lost before
Some neighbor jogs or walks a poodle past.
To fetch my paper isn't all that hard
To ask—but who will pick my ripening figs?
The distance to my tree, across the yard,
Might just as well be here to Alpha Cyg.
Some mornings it's as if I'm three years old,
My parents sleeping off a drunk in bed.
The stove's off limits, so my cocoa's cold.
I want to hear the Sunday funnies read!
Dear Lord, forgive me my impatient soul:
Remind me I was never in control.

MY GREAT-AUNT GRACE

Grace Ellen Glynn Wild (1894–1941)

I would be lying where she lies if not for the grace of God.
That is the price for trying to drink a whole case of God.

She fell down a flight of stairs and fractured her skull.
"Complications of alcoholism," wrote the coroner in the space of God.

What shame did she bring her sisters, who would not claim the corpse?
She lay in the morgue six months. Slow is the pace of God.

When I was fat with cash, I tried to buy her a stone—
Forbidden in that potter's field, which is not a place of God.

I stare at the wedding photo, my great-aunt's little fox-face
Radiant as if she had just glimpsed the face of God.

She married a sailor, was saved from a waitressing job—
But soon it was clear he was not from a race of gods.

"Straighten up or you'll end up on Dover Street"—
So warned the nuns of Boston, who were the chaste of God.

Her last address was a cold-water rooming house on Dover Street.
Carried out on a stretcher drunk, to the disgrace of God.

I carry her disease as I carry her middle name.
Written on paper, not stone, it cannot be effaced by God.

THORN-HEDGE VILLANELLE

Is getting sober like the act it takes
to free a kingdom from a magic spell?
The thorn-hedge crumbling as the sleepers wake

and century-old bread begins to bake
and dogs scratch fleas and horses jingle bells
with you there marveling: *that's* all it takes?

Ex-students text you their sobriety dates
who used to workshop blackout villanelles:
oh what a miracle, to see them wake

to sweet lives free of vomit and the shakes.
You unkissed liquor, and a thorn-hedge fell,
one bumbling action all it ever takes.

And, at the risk of sounding like a flake,
you wonder if the genes inside a cell
can mend themselves when family members wake:

the latest news about your cousin makes
four in your generation spared the hell
that took your elders as a thorn-hedge takes
a kingdom where all die before they wake.

AS IF

As if the corpse behind the crime scene tape
Got up and took a bow where it dropped dead;
As if I got a phone call from the grave
And asked its occupant to share my bed.
Nine years ago, we fought and split apart
With our beloved city underwater.
I turned to short-term lovers in the dark;
You moved in with a southern judge's daughter.
I have to pinch myself to prove you're back,
Though balder, ten pounds thinner, better dressed—
As if the universe had jumped a track,
No hurricane, no choices second-guessed.
At times my ears pick up the strangest sound,
As if the dead were clapping underground.

THE SCREAM

I used to have a scream stuck in my throat
No matter what I did to jam it down:
Unswallowed pill on which I used to choke

No matter how much alcohol or smoke
I flung at it to try to wash it down.
I used to have a scream stuck in my throat:

Teakettle steam about to sing its note
Or seam of lava barely pressured down.
In desperation, I would sometimes choke

On random cocks to give the thing a poke.
Like tamping pipe tobacco farther down—
But still I had a scream stuck in my throat.

Not like a scream in nightmares, where no mote
Of sound escapes though monsters hunt you down:
In dreams, you *want* to scream, but still you choke.

This monster was still there when I awoke;
No earthly weaponry could bring it down,
Those years I had a scream stuck in my throat
Until I spoke my truth and did not choke.

CPSIA information can be obtained
at www.ICGtesting.com
Printed in the USA
LVHW031949200220
647649LV00004B/422